Cooking with Citrus: 50 Refreshing Recipes

By: Kelly Johnson

Table of Contents

- Lemon Basil Chicken
- Orange Glazed Salmon
- Lime Ceviche
- Lemon Garlic Shrimp
- Orange Roasted Chicken
- Lemon Avocado Salad
- Key Lime Pie
- Orange Sorbet
- Lemon Poppy Seed Muffins
- Grapefruit and Fennel Salad
- Lemon Herb Grilled Vegetables
- Lime and Coconut Rice
- Orange Carrot Soup
- Lemon Sorbet
- Lemon Ricotta Pancakes
- Citrus-Marinated Tofu
- Lemon Ginger Dressing
- Orange and Beet Salad
- Lemonade Popsicles
- Lime Chicken Tacos
- Lemon Blueberry Scones
- Orange Chicken Stir-Fry
- Citrus BBQ Sauce
- Lemon Curd
- Orange and Avocado Toast
- Lemon Cream Cheese Frosting
- Grapefruit Glazed Chicken
- Orange Panna Cotta
- Lemon Poppy Seed Cake
- Lime and Mango Salsa
- Lemon and Cucumber Fizz
- Blood Orange Sorbet
- Orange Almond Cake
- Lemon Risotto
- Orange and Clove Poached Pears

- Lemon and Basil Ice Cream
- Lime Coconut Bars
- Orange and Ginger Beef Stir-Fry
- Lemon Thyme Grilled Salmon
- Lime Margarita Chicken
- Lemon Glazed Donuts
- Blood Orange Salad with Goat Cheese
- Orange-Infused Olive Oil Cake
- Lime and Kiwi Smoothie
- Lemon-Lavender Shortbread Cookies
- Tangerine Shrimp Scampi
- Lemon-Mint Quinoa Salad
- Citrus Zest Chicken Wings
- Lemon Ginger Chicken Soup
- Orange Chocolate Mousse

Lemon Basil Chicken

Ingredients:

- 4 boneless, skinless chicken breasts
- 1 tbsp olive oil
- 2 cloves garlic, minced
- 1 lemon, zest and juice
- 1/4 cup fresh basil, chopped
- Salt and pepper to taste

Instructions:

1. Preheat the oven to 180°C (350°F).
2. Heat olive oil in a pan over medium heat. Add garlic and sauté for 1 minute.
3. Season chicken breasts with salt and pepper, then cook in the pan until browned, about 4-5 minutes per side.
4. Transfer the chicken to a baking dish and drizzle with lemon juice and zest.
5. Bake for 20-25 minutes until the chicken is cooked through.
6. Garnish with fresh basil before serving.

Orange Glazed Salmon

Ingredients:

- 4 salmon fillets
- 1/2 cup orange juice
- 2 tbsp honey
- 1 tbsp soy sauce
- 1 tsp grated ginger
- 1/2 tsp garlic powder
- Salt and pepper to taste

Instructions:

1. Preheat the oven to 200°C (400°F).
2. Mix orange juice, honey, soy sauce, ginger, and garlic powder in a bowl.
3. Season salmon fillets with salt and pepper and place on a baking sheet.
4. Pour the glaze over the salmon fillets.
5. Bake for 12-15 minutes until the salmon is cooked through and flaky.
6. Serve with extra glaze and garnish with orange slices.

Lime Ceviche

Ingredients:

- 1 lb fresh white fish (like tilapia or snapper), cut into small cubes
- 1/2 cup fresh lime juice
- 1/4 cup red onion, finely chopped
- 1/2 cucumber, diced
- 1/2 cup cilantro, chopped
- 1 jalapeño, finely chopped (optional)
- Salt and pepper to taste

Instructions:

1. In a bowl, combine fish cubes and lime juice. Let it marinate in the refrigerator for 1-2 hours until the fish turns opaque.
2. Add red onion, cucumber, cilantro, and jalapeño (if using).
3. Stir gently to combine, and season with salt and pepper to taste.
4. Serve chilled with tortilla chips or over lettuce.

Lemon Garlic Shrimp

Ingredients:

- 1 lb large shrimp, peeled and deveined
- 2 tbsp olive oil
- 4 cloves garlic, minced
- 1 lemon, zest and juice
- 1 tbsp parsley, chopped
- Salt and pepper to taste

Instructions:

1. Heat olive oil in a pan over medium heat. Add garlic and sauté for 1 minute.
2. Add shrimp to the pan and cook for 2-3 minutes per side until pink and cooked through.
3. Stir in lemon juice, zest, parsley, salt, and pepper.
4. Serve immediately over pasta or with a side of vegetables.

Orange Roasted Chicken

Ingredients:

- 1 whole chicken (about 3-4 lbs)
- 2 oranges, quartered
- 1 tbsp olive oil
- 2 cloves garlic, minced
- 1 tsp thyme
- 1/2 tsp paprika
- Salt and pepper to taste

Instructions:

1. Preheat the oven to 200°C (400°F).
2. Rub the chicken with olive oil, garlic, thyme, paprika, salt, and pepper.
3. Stuff the chicken cavity with quartered oranges.
4. Roast the chicken for 1 to 1.5 hours, or until the internal temperature reaches 75°C (165°F).
5. Let the chicken rest for 10 minutes before carving. Serve with roasted vegetables.

Lemon Avocado Salad

Ingredients:

- 2 ripe avocados, diced
- 1 cucumber, diced
- 1/2 red onion, thinly sliced
- 1/4 cup fresh parsley, chopped
- 1 lemon, juice and zest
- 2 tbsp olive oil
- Salt and pepper to taste

Instructions:

1. In a large bowl, combine avocado, cucumber, red onion, and parsley.
2. Drizzle with lemon juice and olive oil.
3. Toss gently, and season with salt and pepper.
4. Serve immediately as a side or light lunch.

Key Lime Pie

Ingredients:

For the crust:

- 1 1/2 cups graham cracker crumbs
- 1/4 cup sugar
- 1/2 cup butter, melted

For the filling:

- 1 can (397g) sweetened condensed milk
- 1/2 cup fresh key lime juice
- 3 large egg yolks
- Whipped cream for topping

Instructions:

1. Preheat the oven to 180°C (350°F).
2. Mix graham cracker crumbs, sugar, and melted butter. Press into a pie dish and bake for 10 minutes.
3. In a bowl, whisk together condensed milk, lime juice, and egg yolks.
4. Pour the mixture into the baked crust and bake for 15 minutes until set.
5. Let cool, refrigerate for at least 2 hours, and top with whipped cream before serving.

Orange Sorbet

Ingredients:

- 4 oranges, juiced
- 1/2 cup water
- 1/2 cup sugar
- 1 tbsp orange zest

Instructions:

1. In a saucepan, combine water and sugar. Heat over low heat until sugar dissolves.
2. Add orange juice and zest, stir, and let the mixture cool.
3. Pour the mixture into an ice cream maker and churn according to the manufacturer's instructions.
4. Freeze until firm, then serve.

Lemon Poppy Seed Muffins

Ingredients:

- 1 1/2 cups all-purpose flour
- 1/2 cup sugar
- 1/2 tsp baking powder
- 1/2 tsp baking soda
- 1/4 tsp salt
- 2 tbsp poppy seeds
- 1/2 cup sour cream
- 1/4 cup lemon juice
- 2 eggs
- 1/4 cup butter, melted
- 1 tsp lemon zest

Instructions:

1. Preheat the oven to 180°C (350°F) and grease a muffin tin.
2. In a bowl, mix flour, sugar, baking powder, baking soda, salt, and poppy seeds.
3. In another bowl, whisk together sour cream, lemon juice, eggs, melted butter, and lemon zest.
4. Stir the wet ingredients into the dry ingredients.
5. Fill muffin cups and bake for 18-20 minutes or until a toothpick comes out clean.

Grapefruit and Fennel Salad

Ingredients:

- 2 grapefruits, peeled and segmented
- 1 fennel bulb, thinly sliced
- 1/4 red onion, thinly sliced
- 2 tbsp olive oil
- 1 tbsp white wine vinegar
- Salt and pepper to taste
- 1/4 cup fresh mint leaves, chopped

Instructions:

1. In a large bowl, combine grapefruit segments, fennel, and red onion.
2. In a small bowl, whisk together olive oil, vinegar, salt, and pepper.
3. Drizzle dressing over the salad and toss gently.
4. Garnish with chopped mint leaves and serve chilled.

Lemon Herb Grilled Vegetables

Ingredients:

- 1 zucchini, sliced
- 1 red bell pepper, sliced
- 1 yellow squash, sliced
- 1 red onion, sliced
- 2 tbsp olive oil
- 2 tbsp lemon juice
- 1 tsp dried oregano
- 1/2 tsp garlic powder
- Salt and pepper to taste

Instructions:

1. Preheat the grill to medium-high heat.
2. Toss vegetables with olive oil, lemon juice, oregano, garlic powder, salt, and pepper.
3. Grill vegetables for 4-5 minutes per side, until tender and slightly charred.
4. Serve warm as a side dish or in wraps.

Lime and Coconut Rice

Ingredients:

- 1 cup jasmine rice
- 1 1/2 cups coconut milk
- 1/2 cup water
- 1 lime, juiced and zested
- 1 tbsp sugar
- 1/4 tsp salt

Instructions:

1. Rinse rice under cold water until the water runs clear.
2. In a saucepan, combine coconut milk, water, lime juice, lime zest, sugar, and salt. Bring to a boil.
3. Add rice, stir, reduce heat to low, cover, and cook for 15-20 minutes until rice is tender.
4. Fluff with a fork and serve as a side dish.

Orange Carrot Soup

Ingredients:

- 4 large carrots, peeled and chopped
- 1 orange, juiced and zested
- 1 onion, chopped
- 2 cloves garlic, minced
- 3 cups vegetable broth
- 1 tsp cumin
- 1 tbsp olive oil
- Salt and pepper to taste

Instructions:

1. Heat olive oil in a large pot and sauté onion and garlic until soft.
2. Add carrots, cumin, vegetable broth, orange juice, and zest. Bring to a boil.
3. Reduce heat and simmer for 20-25 minutes until carrots are tender.
4. Blend soup with an immersion blender until smooth.
5. Season with salt and pepper to taste, and serve warm.

Lemon Sorbet

Ingredients:

- 1 cup lemon juice (about 4 lemons)
- 1 1/2 cups water
- 1 cup sugar
- 1/2 tsp lemon zest

Instructions:

1. In a saucepan, combine water and sugar over medium heat, stirring until sugar dissolves. Let cool.
2. Add lemon juice and zest to the syrup mixture, stir to combine.
3. Pour the mixture into an ice cream maker and churn according to the manufacturer's instructions.
4. Transfer to a container and freeze until firm. Serve cold.

Lemon Ricotta Pancakes

Ingredients:

- 1 cup ricotta cheese
- 1 cup all-purpose flour
- 2 eggs
- 1/4 cup milk
- 1 tbsp lemon zest
- 2 tbsp lemon juice
- 2 tbsp sugar
- 1 tsp baking powder
- 1/2 tsp vanilla extract
- Butter or oil for cooking

Instructions:

1. In a bowl, whisk together ricotta, eggs, milk, lemon zest, lemon juice, sugar, and vanilla.
2. In another bowl, mix flour and baking powder. Add to the wet ingredients and stir until combined.
3. Heat a skillet over medium heat and add butter or oil. Pour batter onto the skillet and cook for 2-3 minutes per side until golden brown.
4. Serve with maple syrup or fresh berries.

Citrus-Marinated Tofu

Ingredients:

- 1 block firm tofu, pressed and sliced
- 1 orange, juiced
- 1 lime, juiced
- 1 tbsp soy sauce
- 1 tbsp olive oil
- 1 clove garlic, minced
- 1/2 tsp cumin
- Salt and pepper to taste

Instructions:

1. In a bowl, whisk together orange juice, lime juice, soy sauce, olive oil, garlic, cumin, salt, and pepper.
2. Marinate tofu slices in the citrus mixture for at least 30 minutes.
3. Heat a skillet over medium heat and cook tofu for 3-4 minutes per side until golden brown.
4. Serve with rice or vegetables.

Lemon Ginger Dressing

Ingredients:

- 2 tbsp fresh lemon juice
- 1 tsp lemon zest
- 1 tbsp grated ginger
- 1 tbsp honey
- 1/4 cup olive oil
- Salt and pepper to taste

Instructions:

1. In a bowl, whisk together lemon juice, lemon zest, grated ginger, and honey.
2. Slowly drizzle in olive oil while whisking to emulsify.
3. Season with salt and pepper to taste.
4. Use as a dressing for salads, roasted vegetables, or grilled meats.

Orange and Beet Salad

Ingredients:

- 2 oranges, peeled and segmented
- 2 medium beets, roasted and sliced
- 1/4 cup goat cheese, crumbled
- 1/4 cup walnuts, toasted
- 2 tbsp olive oil
- 1 tbsp balsamic vinegar
- Salt and pepper to taste

Instructions:

1. Arrange beet slices and orange segments on a platter.
2. Drizzle with olive oil and balsamic vinegar, and season with salt and pepper.
3. Sprinkle with goat cheese and toasted walnuts.
4. Serve immediately as a refreshing side dish or appetizer.

Lemonade Popsicles

Ingredients:

- 2 cups lemonade
- 1 tbsp honey (optional)
- 1/2 cup water
- Fresh mint leaves (optional)

Instructions:

1. Mix lemonade, water, and honey (if using) in a bowl until well combined.
2. Pour the mixture into popsicle molds and add a few fresh mint leaves if desired.
3. Insert sticks and freeze for at least 4 hours or until solid.
4. Remove from molds and enjoy!

Lime Chicken Tacos

Ingredients:

- 500g chicken breasts, cooked and shredded
- 1/4 cup lime juice
- 1 tbsp olive oil
- 1 tsp cumin
- 1 tsp chili powder
- Salt and pepper to taste
- 8 small tortillas
- 1/2 cup shredded lettuce
- 1/4 cup diced tomato
- 1/4 cup crumbled queso fresco

Instructions:

1. In a bowl, mix lime juice, olive oil, cumin, chili powder, salt, and pepper.
2. Toss shredded chicken in the lime marinade and let it sit for 10 minutes.
3. Warm tortillas and fill with seasoned chicken, lettuce, tomato, and queso fresco.
4. Serve immediately with lime wedges on the side.

Lemon Blueberry Scones

Ingredients:

- 2 cups all-purpose flour
- 1/4 cup sugar
- 1 tbsp baking powder
- 1/2 tsp salt
- 1/2 cup cold butter, cubed
- 1/2 cup heavy cream
- 1 egg
- 1 tbsp lemon zest
- 1/2 cup blueberries

Instructions:

1. Preheat the oven to 200°C (400°F).
2. In a large bowl, combine flour, sugar, baking powder, and salt.
3. Cut in the butter until the mixture resembles coarse crumbs.
4. In a separate bowl, whisk together heavy cream, egg, and lemon zest.
5. Add the wet ingredients to the dry ingredients, mixing until just combined. Gently fold in blueberries.
6. Shape dough into a circle, cut into wedges, and bake for 15-20 minutes or until golden brown.

Orange Chicken Stir-Fry

Ingredients:

- 500g chicken breast, sliced
- 1 orange, juiced and zest
- 2 tbsp soy sauce
- 1 tbsp rice vinegar
- 1 tbsp honey
- 2 tbsp olive oil
- 1 red bell pepper, sliced
- 1 onion, sliced
- 1/2 cup snap peas
- 1 tbsp cornstarch mixed with 2 tbsp water

Instructions:

1. In a bowl, whisk together orange juice, soy sauce, rice vinegar, honey, and cornstarch mixture.
2. Heat olive oil in a pan and sauté chicken slices until cooked through.
3. Remove chicken and set aside. In the same pan, cook bell pepper, onion, and snap peas for 3-4 minutes.
4. Add chicken back to the pan and pour in the orange sauce. Cook until the sauce thickens and coats the chicken and vegetables.
5. Serve over rice or noodles.

Citrus BBQ Sauce

Ingredients:

- 1 cup orange juice
- 1/2 cup lemon juice
- 1/4 cup honey
- 1/2 cup ketchup
- 1 tbsp soy sauce
- 1 tbsp Dijon mustard
- 1/2 tsp garlic powder
- Salt and pepper to taste

Instructions:

1. In a saucepan, combine orange juice, lemon juice, honey, ketchup, soy sauce, mustard, and garlic powder.
2. Bring to a simmer over medium heat and cook for 15-20 minutes until thickened.
3. Season with salt and pepper to taste.
4. Brush onto grilled meats or use as a dipping sauce.

Lemon Curd

Ingredients:

- 4 large eggs
- 1/2 cup sugar
- 1/2 cup fresh lemon juice
- 2 tbsp lemon zest
- 1/4 cup butter, cubed

Instructions:

1. In a heatproof bowl, whisk together eggs, sugar, lemon juice, and lemon zest.
2. Set the bowl over a pot of simmering water and whisk constantly until the mixture thickens (about 10 minutes).
3. Remove from heat and whisk in butter until smooth.
4. Cool to room temperature, then refrigerate. Use for tarts, cakes, or toast.

Orange and Avocado Toast

Ingredients:

- 2 slices of whole grain or sourdough bread
- 1 ripe avocado, mashed
- 1/2 orange, peeled and segmented
- Salt and pepper to taste
- 1 tbsp olive oil (optional)

Instructions:

1. Toast the bread until golden brown.
2. Spread mashed avocado evenly on the toast.
3. Arrange orange segments on top of the avocado.
4. Drizzle with olive oil, if desired, and season with salt and pepper.
5. Serve immediately for a refreshing, light breakfast.

Lemon Cream Cheese Frosting

Ingredients:

- 8 oz cream cheese, softened
- 1/4 cup unsalted butter, softened
- 2 cups powdered sugar
- 1 tbsp fresh lemon juice
- 1 tsp lemon zest
- 1/2 tsp vanilla extract

Instructions:

1. Beat cream cheese and butter together until smooth and fluffy.
2. Gradually add powdered sugar, mixing until well incorporated.
3. Stir in lemon juice, lemon zest, and vanilla.
4. Frost cakes, cupcakes, or cookies with this tangy, creamy frosting.

Grapefruit Glazed Chicken

Ingredients:

- 4 boneless, skinless chicken breasts
- 1 grapefruit, juiced and zested
- 1 tbsp honey
- 1 tbsp soy sauce
- 1 tbsp olive oil
- 1 clove garlic, minced
- Salt and pepper to taste

Instructions:

1. In a small saucepan, combine grapefruit juice, honey, soy sauce, olive oil, garlic, salt, and pepper.
2. Bring to a simmer and cook for 5-7 minutes until thickened into a glaze.
3. Season chicken breasts with salt and pepper and cook in a pan until browned and cooked through.
4. Brush the grapefruit glaze onto the chicken in the last few minutes of cooking.
5. Serve with extra glaze and garnish with grapefruit zest.

Orange Panna Cotta

Ingredients:

- 1 cup heavy cream
- 1 cup whole milk
- 1/2 cup sugar
- 1 tbsp orange zest
- 1/2 cup orange juice
- 1 tsp vanilla extract
- 2 tsp gelatin powder
- 2 tbsp water

Instructions:

1. In a small bowl, dissolve gelatin in water and let sit for 5 minutes.
2. In a saucepan, heat cream, milk, sugar, and orange zest over medium heat until the sugar dissolves.
3. Remove from heat and stir in orange juice, vanilla, and gelatin mixture until smooth.
4. Pour into ramekins and refrigerate for 4 hours or until set.
5. Serve with a fresh orange segment or citrus syrup.

Lemon Poppy Seed Cake

Ingredients:

- 2 cups all-purpose flour
- 1 1/2 cups sugar
- 1/2 cup butter, softened
- 3 large eggs
- 1 cup milk
- 1 tbsp lemon zest
- 2 tbsp lemon juice
- 2 tbsp poppy seeds
- 1 tsp baking powder
- 1/2 tsp baking soda
- 1/4 tsp salt

Instructions:

1. Preheat the oven to 180°C (350°F). Grease and flour a cake pan.
2. In a bowl, mix flour, baking powder, baking soda, salt, and poppy seeds.
3. In a separate bowl, cream butter and sugar together until light and fluffy.
4. Add eggs one at a time, followed by lemon juice, zest, and milk. Mix until combined.
5. Gradually add the dry ingredients and mix until smooth.
6. Pour batter into the prepared pan and bake for 30-35 minutes, or until a toothpick comes out clean.
7. Cool in the pan for 10 minutes, then transfer to a wire rack to cool completely.

Lime and Mango Salsa

Ingredients:

- 1 ripe mango, diced
- 1/2 red onion, finely chopped
- 1 red bell pepper, diced
- 1/4 cup cilantro, chopped
- 1 lime, juiced
- 1 small jalapeño, minced (optional)
- Salt and pepper to taste

Instructions:

1. In a bowl, combine mango, onion, bell pepper, cilantro, and jalapeño (if using).
2. Add lime juice and stir well.
3. Season with salt and pepper to taste.
4. Serve with tortilla chips, grilled meats, or as a topping for tacos.

Lemon and Cucumber Fizz

Ingredients:

- 1 cucumber, sliced
- 1 lemon, juiced
- 1 tbsp honey (optional)
- 2 cups sparkling water
- Ice cubes

Instructions:

1. In a pitcher, combine lemon juice, cucumber slices, and honey.
2. Muddle the ingredients gently with a muddler or the back of a spoon to release the cucumber's juices.
3. Fill glasses with ice cubes and pour the lemon-cucumber mixture over the ice.
4. Top with sparkling water and stir well.
5. Serve chilled with extra cucumber slices as garnish.

Blood Orange Sorbet

Ingredients:

- 4 blood oranges, juiced
- 1/2 cup sugar
- 1 cup water
- 1 tbsp lemon juice

Instructions:

1. In a saucepan, combine water and sugar, and heat over medium heat until the sugar dissolves.
2. Let the syrup cool, then mix in the blood orange juice and lemon juice.
3. Pour the mixture into an ice cream maker and churn according to the manufacturer's instructions.
4. Freeze the sorbet for 2-3 hours before serving.

Orange Almond Cake

Ingredients:

- 2 cups almond flour
- 1 cup sugar
- 1/4 cup orange juice
- 3 large eggs
- 1 tsp vanilla extract
- 1/2 tsp baking powder
- 1/4 tsp salt

Instructions:

1. Preheat the oven to 180°C (350°F). Grease a cake pan.
2. In a bowl, mix almond flour, sugar, baking powder, and salt.
3. In another bowl, whisk eggs, orange juice, and vanilla extract.
4. Combine the wet and dry ingredients, stirring until smooth.
5. Pour the batter into the prepared pan and bake for 25-30 minutes, or until a toothpick comes out clean.
6. Cool in the pan for 10 minutes, then transfer to a wire rack to cool completely.

Lemon Risotto

Ingredients:

- 1 cup Arborio rice
- 1 tbsp olive oil
- 1/2 onion, chopped
- 2 cloves garlic, minced
- 4 cups vegetable broth, heated
- 1/2 cup white wine
- 1 lemon, juiced and zest
- 1/4 cup Parmesan cheese, grated
- Salt and pepper to taste

Instructions:

1. Heat olive oil in a pan and sauté onion and garlic until soft.
2. Add Arborio rice and cook for 1-2 minutes, stirring constantly.
3. Pour in white wine and cook until absorbed.
4. Gradually add the warm broth, one ladle at a time, stirring constantly until the liquid is absorbed before adding more.
5. Continue this process until the rice is tender, about 20 minutes.
6. Stir in lemon juice, zest, Parmesan cheese, and season with salt and pepper. Serve immediately.

Orange and Clove Poached Pears

Ingredients:

- 4 pears, peeled and cored
- 2 cups orange juice
- 1/2 cup sugar
- 1 cinnamon stick
- 4 cloves
- 1 tbsp lemon juice

Instructions:

1. In a saucepan, combine orange juice, sugar, cinnamon stick, cloves, and lemon juice.
2. Bring to a boil, then reduce to a simmer.
3. Add the pears and cook for 20-25 minutes, turning occasionally, until tender.
4. Remove the pears and let the syrup reduce to a thicker consistency, about 10 minutes.
5. Serve the pears with a drizzle of syrup.

Lemon and Basil Ice Cream

Ingredients:

- 1 cup heavy cream
- 1 cup whole milk
- 1/2 cup sugar
- 1/4 cup lemon juice
- 2 tsp lemon zest
- 1/2 cup fresh basil leaves, chopped

Instructions:

1. In a saucepan, combine milk, cream, sugar, lemon juice, and lemon zest. Heat over medium heat until sugar is dissolved.
2. Remove from heat and stir in chopped basil.
3. Let the mixture steep for 15-20 minutes, then strain out the basil.
4. Cool the mixture, then churn in an ice cream maker according to the manufacturer's instructions.
5. Freeze for 2-3 hours before serving.

Lime Coconut Bars

Ingredients:

- 1 1/2 cups graham cracker crumbs
- 1/4 cup sugar
- 1/2 cup butter, melted
- 1 can (400g) sweetened condensed milk
- 1/2 cup shredded coconut
- 1/4 cup lime juice
- 1 tbsp lime zest

Instructions:

1. Preheat the oven to 180°C (350°F).
2. Mix graham cracker crumbs, sugar, and melted butter in a bowl, then press into a greased baking dish.
3. In a separate bowl, combine sweetened condensed milk, shredded coconut, lime juice, and lime zest.
4. Pour the mixture over the crust and bake for 20-25 minutes, or until set.
5. Let cool, then cut into bars.

Orange and Ginger Beef Stir-Fry

Ingredients:

- 500g beef sirloin, thinly sliced
- 1 orange, juiced and zested
- 1 tbsp soy sauce
- 1 tbsp ginger, grated
- 1/2 tsp garlic powder
- 1 tbsp olive oil
- 1/2 cup bell peppers, sliced
- 1/2 cup snap peas
- 2 tbsp sesame oil

Instructions:

1. Heat olive oil in a skillet over medium heat and cook the beef slices until browned, about 3-4 minutes.
2. Add bell peppers, snap peas, ginger, garlic powder, and cook for an additional 2-3 minutes.
3. Stir in orange juice, zest, soy sauce, and sesame oil.
4. Cook for 1-2 more minutes and serve immediately over rice or noodles.

Lemon Thyme Grilled Salmon

Ingredients:

- 4 salmon fillets
- 2 tbsp olive oil
- 1 lemon, juiced and zest
- 2 sprigs fresh thyme
- 2 cloves garlic, minced
- Salt and pepper to taste

Instructions:

1. Preheat the grill to medium-high heat.
2. In a small bowl, whisk together olive oil, lemon juice, zest, garlic, and thyme.
3. Brush the salmon fillets with the lemon-thyme mixture and season with salt and pepper.
4. Grill the salmon for 4-5 minutes per side, until the salmon is cooked through and flakes easily with a fork.
5. Serve immediately, garnished with extra thyme and lemon wedges.

Lime Margarita Chicken

Ingredients:

- 4 boneless, skinless chicken breasts
- 1/4 cup lime juice
- 2 tbsp tequila (optional)
- 2 tbsp olive oil
- 1 tbsp honey
- 2 cloves garlic, minced
- 1/2 tsp chili powder
- Salt and pepper to taste

Instructions:

1. In a bowl, whisk together lime juice, tequila, olive oil, honey, garlic, chili powder, salt, and pepper.
2. Place chicken breasts in a zip-lock bag or shallow dish and pour marinade over them. Seal and refrigerate for at least 1 hour.
3. Preheat the grill to medium heat.
4. Grill the chicken for 5-7 minutes per side, until the internal temperature reaches 75°C (165°F).
5. Serve with a side of rice or grilled vegetables.

Lemon Glazed Donuts

Ingredients:

For the donuts:

- 1 1/2 cups all-purpose flour
- 1/2 cup sugar
- 1 1/2 tsp baking powder
- 1/2 tsp salt
- 1/2 tsp baking soda
- 2/3 cup buttermilk
- 2 large eggs
- 1/4 cup unsalted butter, melted
- 1 tsp vanilla extract
- 1 tbsp lemon zest

For the glaze:

- 1 cup powdered sugar
- 2 tbsp lemon juice
- 1/2 tsp lemon zest

Instructions:

1. Preheat the oven to 180°C (350°F) and grease a donut pan.
2. In a bowl, whisk together flour, sugar, baking powder, salt, and baking soda.
3. In another bowl, combine buttermilk, eggs, melted butter, vanilla extract, and lemon zest.
4. Add the wet ingredients to the dry ingredients and mix until combined.
5. Spoon the batter into the donut pan and bake for 12-15 minutes, until a toothpick comes out clean.
6. For the glaze, whisk together powdered sugar, lemon juice, and zest.
7. Once the donuts are cool, dip them into the glaze and set them aside to dry.

Blood Orange Salad with Goat Cheese

Ingredients:

- 2 blood oranges, peeled and segmented
- 1/4 red onion, thinly sliced
- 1/4 cup goat cheese, crumbled
- 1/4 cup walnuts, toasted
- 2 cups mixed greens (arugula or spinach)
- 2 tbsp olive oil
- 1 tbsp balsamic vinegar
- Salt and pepper to taste

Instructions:

1. In a large bowl, combine blood orange segments, red onion, goat cheese, walnuts, and mixed greens.
2. In a small bowl, whisk together olive oil, balsamic vinegar, salt, and pepper.
3. Drizzle the dressing over the salad and toss gently.
4. Serve immediately as a refreshing side dish or light lunch.

Orange-Infused Olive Oil Cake

Ingredients:

- 1 1/2 cups all-purpose flour
- 1/2 tsp baking powder
- 1/4 tsp baking soda
- 1/2 tsp salt
- 1/2 cup extra virgin olive oil
- 1 cup sugar
- 3 large eggs
- 1/2 cup orange juice
- 1 tbsp orange zest
- 1 tsp vanilla extract

Instructions:

1. Preheat the oven to 180°C (350°F) and grease a bundt pan.
2. In a bowl, whisk together flour, baking powder, baking soda, and salt.
3. In another bowl, beat olive oil, sugar, eggs, orange juice, zest, and vanilla extract until smooth.
4. Gradually add the dry ingredients to the wet mixture and stir until just combined.
5. Pour the batter into the bundt pan and bake for 30-35 minutes, or until a toothpick comes out clean.
6. Cool the cake in the pan for 10 minutes, then transfer to a wire rack to cool completely.

Lime and Kiwi Smoothie

Ingredients:

- 2 ripe kiwis, peeled and chopped
- 1 lime, juiced
- 1/2 cup coconut water or regular water
- 1/2 cup ice
- 1 tbsp honey (optional)

Instructions:

1. In a blender, combine kiwis, lime juice, coconut water, ice, and honey (if desired).
2. Blend until smooth and creamy.
3. Pour into a glass and serve chilled.

Lemon-Lavender Shortbread Cookies

Ingredients:

- 1 cup unsalted butter, softened
- 1/2 cup powdered sugar
- 2 cups all-purpose flour
- 1 tsp lemon zest
- 1 tbsp dried lavender flowers
- 1/2 tsp vanilla extract
- Pinch of salt

Instructions:

1. Preheat the oven to 180°C (350°F) and line a baking sheet with parchment paper.
2. In a bowl, cream together the butter and powdered sugar until light and fluffy.
3. Add flour, lemon zest, lavender, vanilla, and salt, mixing until a dough forms.
4. Roll the dough out between two sheets of parchment paper to about 1/4 inch thickness.
5. Cut into shapes (like circles or squares) and place on the prepared baking sheet.
6. Bake for 12-15 minutes, or until the edges are golden.
7. Let the cookies cool before serving.

Tangerine Shrimp Scampi

Ingredients:

- 1 lb large shrimp, peeled and deveined
- 1 tbsp olive oil
- 3 cloves garlic, minced
- 1/2 cup tangerine juice
- 1/4 cup white wine
- 1 tbsp lemon juice
- 1 tsp lemon zest
- 1/2 tsp red pepper flakes (optional)
- 1/4 cup chopped parsley
- Salt and pepper to taste
- 1 lb linguine or pasta of choice

Instructions:

1. Cook the linguine according to package instructions and set aside.
2. Heat olive oil in a large skillet over medium heat. Add garlic and sauté until fragrant, about 1 minute.
3. Add the shrimp to the skillet and cook until pink, about 2-3 minutes per side.
4. Remove shrimp from the skillet and set aside.
5. Pour tangerine juice, white wine, lemon juice, and zest into the skillet, scraping up any bits from the pan. Let simmer for 5 minutes to reduce the sauce slightly.
6. Add the shrimp back to the skillet and toss with the sauce.
7. Stir in parsley and red pepper flakes (if using).
8. Serve the shrimp and sauce over the cooked linguine.

Lemon-Mint Quinoa Salad

Ingredients:

- 1 cup quinoa, cooked and cooled
- 1/2 cup cucumber, diced
- 1/2 cup cherry tomatoes, halved
- 1/4 cup red onion, finely chopped
- 1/4 cup fresh mint, chopped
- 1/4 cup lemon juice
- 2 tbsp olive oil
- Salt and pepper to taste

Instructions:

1. In a large bowl, combine cooked quinoa, cucumber, tomatoes, red onion, and fresh mint.
2. In a small bowl, whisk together lemon juice, olive oil, salt, and pepper.
3. Drizzle the dressing over the quinoa mixture and toss to combine.
4. Chill in the refrigerator for 30 minutes before serving.

Citrus Zest Chicken Wings

Ingredients:

- 12 chicken wings
- 2 tbsp olive oil
- 1 tbsp orange zest
- 1 tbsp lemon zest
- 1 tbsp lime zest
- 2 cloves garlic, minced
- 1 tbsp honey
- Salt and pepper to taste

Instructions:

1. Preheat the oven to 200°C (400°F) and line a baking sheet with parchment paper.
2. In a bowl, mix olive oil, orange zest, lemon zest, lime zest, garlic, honey, salt, and pepper.
3. Toss the chicken wings in the citrus marinade, making sure they are well coated.
4. Place the wings on the prepared baking sheet and bake for 25-30 minutes, flipping halfway through.
5. Serve the wings with your favorite dipping sauce or garnish with extra citrus zest.

Lemon Ginger Chicken Soup

Ingredients:

- 1 lb chicken breast, cooked and shredded
- 6 cups chicken broth
- 1-inch piece of ginger, grated
- 2 carrots, diced
- 2 celery stalks, diced
- 1 onion, chopped
- 1 lemon, juiced and zest
- 2 garlic cloves, minced
- 1 tbsp olive oil
- Salt and pepper to taste

Instructions:

1. Heat olive oil in a large pot over medium heat. Add onion, garlic, carrots, and celery, and sauté for 5 minutes until softened.
2. Add the grated ginger, chicken broth, and shredded chicken. Bring to a simmer.
3. Add lemon juice and zest, then season with salt and pepper.
4. Simmer for 15-20 minutes to allow the flavors to meld.
5. Serve hot, garnished with extra lemon zest or fresh herbs.

Orange Chocolate Mousse

Ingredients:

- 1 cup dark chocolate, chopped
- 1/2 cup heavy cream
- 1/4 cup orange juice
- 1 tsp orange zest
- 2 tbsp powdered sugar
- 1/2 cup whipped cream (for topping)

Instructions:

1. In a heatproof bowl, melt dark chocolate over a double boiler or in the microwave in 30-second intervals, stirring in between.
2. In a saucepan, heat heavy cream and orange juice over medium heat until it begins to simmer.
3. Pour the hot cream into the melted chocolate and stir until smooth.
4. Stir in the orange zest and powdered sugar.
5. Refrigerate the mousse for at least 2 hours, until firm.
6. Serve the mousse topped with whipped cream and extra orange zest.

www.ingramcontent.com/pod-product-compliance
Lightning Source LLC
LaVergne TN
LVHW081508060526
838201LV00056BA/2995